THIRD GRADE GEOGRAPHY
EARTHQUAKES AND VOLCANOES

Volcanic eruptions are
usually preceded by
earthquakes large and small.

EARTHQUAKES

Earthquakes are the shaking, rolling or sudden shock of the earth's surface. They are the Earth's natural means of releasing stress.

A seismograph is an instrument used for recording the intensity and duration of an earthquake.

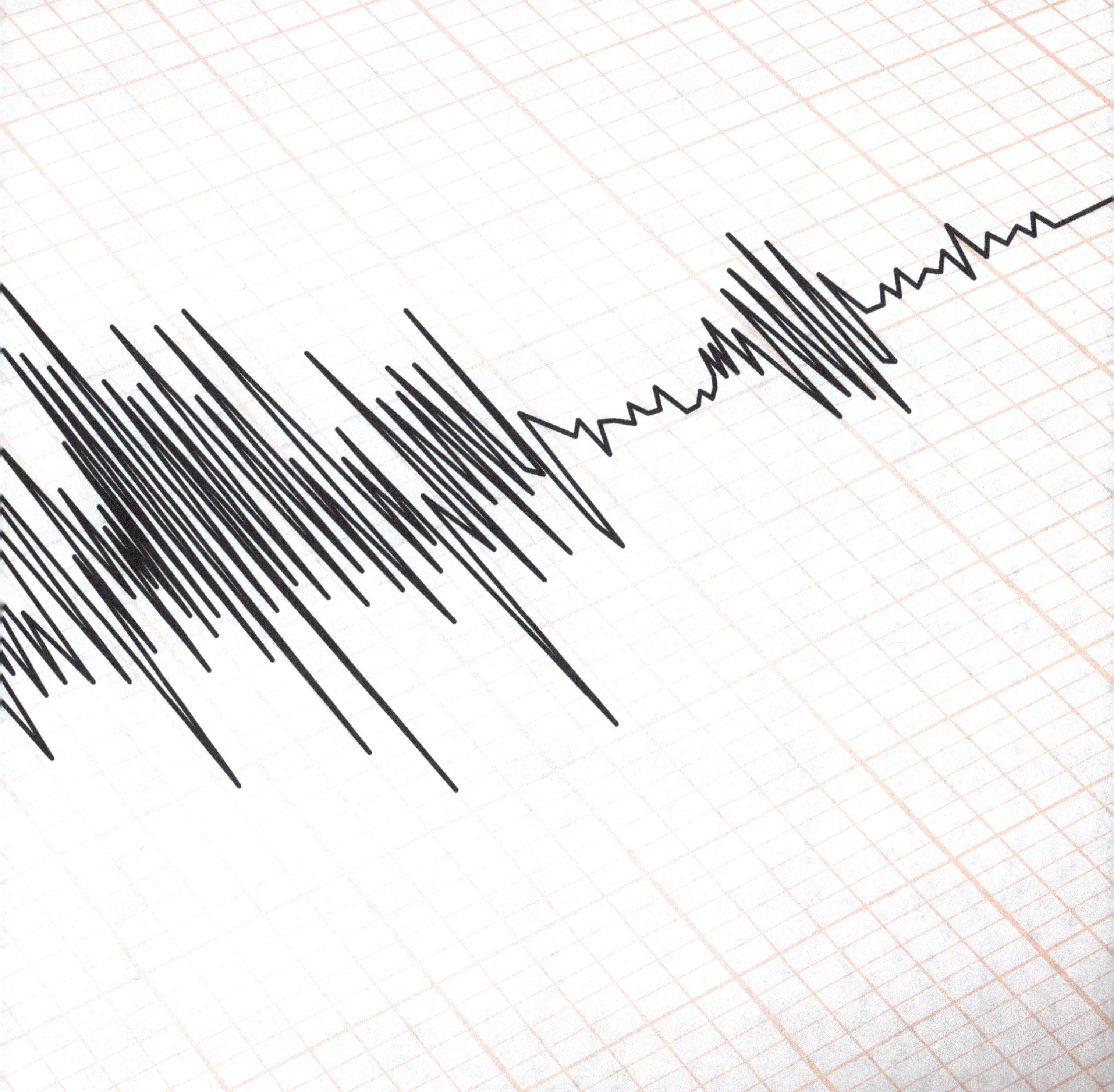

Underneath the Earth's surface lie tectonic plates. When the plates squeeze or stretch, huge rocks form at their edges and the rocks shift with great force, causing an earthquake.

VOLCANOES

Volcanoes are openings in the Earth's surface. When they are active they spew lava, rock, poisonous gases and ash with great power.

The word volcano
originally comes
from the name of
the Roman god
of fire, Vulcan.

Hot liquid rock
under the Earth's
surface is known
as magma, it is
called lava after
it comes out of
a volcano.